Blackrock, Dublin, Dalkey

Along the coast from Booterstown to Killiney

Paintings by Tom Roche

Text by Ken Finlay

Cottage

Publications

First published by Cottage Publications,
an imprint of Laurel Cottage Ltd.
Donaghadee, N. Ireland 2003.
Copyrights Reserved.
© Illustrations Tom Roche 2003
© Text by Ken Finlay 2003
All rights reserved.
No part of this book may be reproduced or stored
on any media without the express written
permission of the publishers.
Design & origination in Northern Ireland.
Printed & bound in Singapore.

ISBN 1 90093534 1

Tom Roche

Tom Roche was born and educated in Dublin. He trained as Graphic Designer and Visualiser before working in advertising in both Dublin and London. He won first place in the 'Sunday Times' book cover awards and in 1966 was awarded a bronze medal for his work by the French Ambassador to Ireland.

In 1971 Tom moved to Kerry with his family to paint full time. He has had many one-man exhibitions in Ireland, and abroad and is a member of the Watercolour Society of Ireland and The Dublin Painting & Sketching Club. He is also a part-time lecturer in The Dun Laoghaire Institute of Art, Design & Technology and in the Grain Store Art Studio, Cabinteely.

Tom presently lives in Dun Laoghaire, County Dublin, with his wife Aisling and can be contacted by e-mail (tomrochestudio@eircom.net).

Ken Finlay

Ken Finlay was born in Dublin, and is the Editor of the weekly free newspaper The Southside People (East).

His interest in the history of Dublin led him to create the website Chapters of Dublin History (www.dublinhistory.net) in which can be found the text of over 50 out of copyright books about Dublin. There are also many general articles about the city and county, photographs and links to other Dublin sites.

He is a member of the Old Dublin Society and of the Dun Laoghaire Borough Historical Society.

Ken lives in Dun Laoghaire with his wife Anne. He can be contacted by e-mail (kfinlay@indigo.ie).

Contents

Beginnings

The main section of this book deals with the period from the 5th century, when Christianity arrived, up to the present day. Most of the information concerns the period after the arrival of the Normans in 1171.

From that time onwards there is written information, nowhere near complete, but enough to give a good idea of what was happening in the coastal strip from Booterstown to Killiney. Since the coming of the railway in the early 19th century those areas have been more closely linked and today they mark the eastern boundary of the newly formed local authority, Dun Laoghaire Rathdown County Council.

Archaeologists who, from 1956-9, sifted through 5,500 year old rubbish heaps on Dalkey Island provided the earliest evidence of people living in our area.

The items found showed that the island was occupied, on and off, for many centuries and that the people had a rich diet gleaned both from the land and the sea.

The small dolmen (a tomb with four upright stones supporting a roof stone) at Cromlech Fields in Ballybrack has been dated to around 4,500 years ago.

The building boom over the last 200 years resulted in the complete destruction of many early sites – some, like the Bulloch Rocking Stone and the dún (fort) from which Dun Laoghaire takes its name, were large and appear on early maps and in drawings, many others were neither marked nor investigated.

But every now and again finds are made which remind us that pre-historic people lived here – a Bronze Age burial unearthed at the Stillorgan Obelisk (1955) contained the skeleton of a woman who had been killed by a head wound; copper axes have been found in Cabinteely and an Iron Age bracelet near Monkstown.

It might be thought that such a small area would have a certain sameness but there is tremendous variation – Dalkey, now one of Ireland's Heritage Towns, was a medieval village, while modern-day Dun Laoghaire is a town which didn't even exist until early in the 19th century.

Only in a few instances have we moved inland, in particular to write about Kill Abbey. Everywhere described is within walking distance of the DART (Dublin Area Rapid Transit) – Kill Abbey is a longer walk but is served by the 46A bus from Dun Laoghaire DART station.

To avoid any confusion 'Dun Laoghaire' is used unless specifically referring to 'Kingstown' or 'Dunleary'.

The confusion arises over the renaming of the town to 'Kingstown' to mark the visit by King George IV in 1821. One hundred years later, as the Irish Free State (Saorstát Éireann) came into existence, the name was changed back to Dún Laoghaire.

They Lived Here

Many people, both famous and infamous, have lived in and around the coastal strip between Booterstown and Killiney. The area is today more popular and more expensive than ever and among those who will doubtless feature on similar lists in the future are Maeve Binchy, Hugh Leonard, Bernard Farrell, Ronnie Drew and Enya. This, however, is a listing of those who lived here once upon a time.

Francis Elrington Ball (1863-1928), Dublin historian. Author of the classic six-volume *A History of the County Dublin* (1902-1920), he lived for a time at Booterstown House.

Samuel Beckett, (1906-1989), Cooldrinagh, Foxrock. Playwright, poet, novelist and member of the French Resistance. Author of *Waiting for Godot, Krapp's Last Tape*, and *Endgame,* Beckett received the Nobel Prize for Literature in 1969. Like James Joyce he left Ireland and wrote highly praised works, which remain largely unread in his native city.

Jem Casey (c. 1880 - ?). For such knowledge as we have of the life and times of the man known as the Bard of Booterstown, humanity is indebted to Flann O'Brien's seminal work of 1939, which brought this hitherto unpublished genius to wider attention. From Casey's other sobriquet 'The Poet Of The Pick' we know his occupation, a navvie, rhyming to the rhythm of his work. However, mere biographical detail fades into triviality compared with the treasure-trove that his oeuvre represents. A sample speaks for itself:

> *When things go wrong and will not come right,*
> *Though you do the best you can,*
> *When life looks black as the hour of night,*
> *A PINT OF PLAIN IS YOUR ONLY MAN.*

Padraig Colum, (1881-1972), lived in Sandycove as a youth (his father was station-master there). Poet, author and dramatist. Author of the lyrics of *She Moved through the Fair*. His first collection of poetry *Wild Earth* was published in 1907. Colum lived in the U.S.A. from 1914 but continued to make extended trips home.

Roger Casement, (1864-1916). Born 29 Lawson Terrace, Sandycove. As a British civil servant he investigated abuse of native workers in the Belgian Congo and on Peruvian rubber plantations. Knighted in 1911. Captured in Kerry after landing from a German submarine (1916). Executed in Pentonville Prison. Re-interred in Glasnevin Cemetery in 1965. Whether he was a homosexual or not still causes debate.

Sir Dominic Corrigan, (1802-1880), built and lived at Inniscorrig, Coliemore Road, Dalkey. Physician. Gave his name to an unusual pulse caused by a disease of the heart – 'Corrigan's Pulse.'

Cyril Cusack, (1910-1993), lived in Sandycove. Actor and writer. Appeared in over 60 Abbey Theatre productions (1932-1945) – greatest acclaim as Christy Mahon in *The Playboy of the Western World*. Successful film actor *Odd Man Out* and *My Left Foot*. Author of three volumes of poetry; *Time Pieces, Poems*, and *Between the Acts*.

Michael Davitt, (1846-1906), lived at Rose Lawn, Military Road, Ballybrack. One-armed (left) Fenian sentenced to 15 years penal servitude in 1870. Released in 1878 he, with Parnell, founded the Land League which fought the land war in which the term 'boycott' came into use.

Lady Arbella Denny, (1707-1792), lived at Lios an Uisce (originally Peafield Cliff) beside the People's Park, Blackrock. Founder of the Magdalen Asylum for Protestant Girls, which was the first such refuge in Ireland. For two decades worked tirelessly to improve the health of children in the Foundling Hospital. Awarded the Freedom of the City. Promoted Irish industry and experimented with breeding silk worms.

Eamon de Valera, (1882-1975), educated and taught at Blackrock College, lived mainly in Blackrock until elected President of Ireland, spent his retirement in Talbot Lodge, Blackrock. Either the saviour or the ruination of Ireland, depending upon which side of the fence you stood, he was both a student and a teacher at Blackrock College (once hiding a revolver behind the altar in the College Chapel).

Fr. Willie Doyle, S.J., (1873-1917), lived in Melrose, Dalkey Avenue. He worked as a Jesuit priest in the poor missions in Dublin and Limerick before the outbreak of WWI. Chaplain to the various Irish Regiments. Awarded a Military Cross for Bravery at the Somme. Either shot or killed by a shell at Passchendaele (June 1917). Recommended for the Victoria Cross. He once wrote, *'I wish to die a martyr's death - but am I willing to live a martyr's life.'*

Lord Edward Fitzgerald, (1763-1798), lived for a time at Frescati Lodge, Blackrock. Wounded during active service in America on the British side at the battle of Eutaw Springs (1781). Influenced by the French Revolution, he visited Paris (1792). Returned to Dublin with his French wife, Pamela, the following year. Eventually decided that only revolution could help Ireland. As leader of the United Irishmen he hoped for French help and Irish volunteers to win the day in May 1798. Fitzgerald, arrested and wounded in Thomas Street, by Major Sirr, died in Newgate Prison on June 4 of that year.

Oliver St. John Gogarty, (1878-1957), sometime resident of the Sandycove Martello Tower and, Seaview, Sorrento Road, Dalkey (1915-1917). Author, poet, politician, surgeon (nose and throat). He is 'Buck Mulligan' in *Ulysses*. Member of the first Senate – captured by Republicans, he escaped by swimming the Liffey, later presenting two swans to the river in gratitude. Author of *An Offering of Swans* (poetry,

1924) and the autobiographical *As I Was Going down Sackville Street.*

Sir John Gray, (1815-1875), had a country retreat at The Strand, Ballybrack. Physician and journalist. Joint owner of the *Freeman's Journal* from 1841 (sole owner from 1850). Strongly supported the Vartry Water Scheme to promote Dublin's sanitary services (until then water was taken from canals). His statue stands on O'Connell Street between those of O'Brien and Larkin.

Monk Gibbon, (1896-1987), lived at Tara Hall, Sandycove Road. Writer, poet, editor. Joined British army at the start of WWI. On leave in Dublin, he saw the murder of Francis Sheehy Skeffington by soldiers in 1916. Author of four volumes of autobiography, plus volumes on poetry, ballet and travel.

Sir Howard Grubb, (1844-1931), lived at De Vesci Terrace and, from 1925-1931, at 13 Longford Terrace (plaque unveiled August 6, 1997). Optical instrument maker. During the First World War, demand was on Grubb's factory to make gunsights and periscopes for the war effort and it was during those years that he perfected the periscope's design. The firm was taken over in 1925 by Sir Charles Parsons and continued in Newcastle as Grubb Parsons until 1984.

Denis Johnston, (1901-1984), lived in retirement on Sorrento Terrace, Dalkey. Playwright, lawyer, academic. First of his nine plays was *The Old Lady Says 'No'* (1928). Received an OBE for his wartime reporting from Africa, Italy and Germany – basis of the book *Nine Rivers to Jordan* (1953).

James Joyce, (1882-1941), lived just about everywhere – including Leoville, 23 Carysfort Avenue, Blackrock; 35 and 103 Strand Road, Sandymount; the Martello Tower, Sandycove. Taught at the Clifton School, Dalkey (1904). Greatest writer of the 20th century according to the literati, considered a 'filthmonger' by those who took grave exception. Living in Paris, being half-blind and employing typesetters who didn't understand English did no damage to his reputation. Best known as the author of *Ulysses.* Up there with Beckett and Shaw as unread, but very famous, authors.

Charles Kickham, (1818-1882), lived at Montpelier Place, Blackrock. Poet, novelist and Fenian. Editor of The Irish People. At 13 a gunpowder explosion damaged his hearing and sight. Sentenced to 14 years in 1865. Released because of poor health after four years. Best remembered for *Knocknagow*, or the *Homes of Tipperary.*

Valentine Brown Lawless, (1773-1853), lived at Maretimo, Blackrock. Irish patriot – he narrowly escaped the fate of his friend Lord Edward Fitzgerald after the 1798 rebellion. Arrested and imprisoned in 1798-99 he later became a British peer. Opposed the Dublin to Kingstown Line until he relented when guaranteed a tunnel would go under his property.

William Edward Hartpole Lecky, (1838-1903), was born at Newtown Park, Blackrock. Historian and writer. His eight-volume *A History of England in the 18th Century (1878-1890)* included much material about Ireland. Turned down the chair of history at Oxford (1892) and was elected MP for the University of Dublin in the same year. He opposed Home Rule.

William Knox Leet, (1833-1898). Born in Dalkey. Soldier who rose through the ranks from Ensign to Major General. As a Major he was awarded the Victoria Cross for his gallant actions during the retreat from Hlobane Mountain (Zulu War, 1879). During the retreat, a lieutenant of the Frontier Light Horse whose horse had been shot from under him was on foot and being closely pursued by the Zulus. He would have been killed had not Major Leet taken him upon his horse and rode with him under fire to safety.

Major John MacBride, (1865-1916), lived at 8

Spencer Villas, Glasthule (1914-1916). Fought against Britain with the Irish Brigade in the Boer War. Married the glamour-girl of Irish Nationalism, Maud Gonne, in Paris (1903) – the later divorce was a major scandal. On his way to Dublin to attend his brother's wedding he came upon the Easter Rising, offered his services, and was appointed second-in-command at Jacob's factory, Bishop Street. Court-martialled and later shot in Kilmainham Jail.

Count John McCormack, (1884-1945), lived at Glena, Rock Road, Booterstown. Lyric tenor and musical superstar, spent a large part of his career in America (took citizenship in 1919). Of his more than 600 records the earlier operatic recordings are regarded as the best. Indifferent actor (*Song O' My Heart*). Made a Papal Count in 1929 because of his work for charity. His performance at the Eucharistic Congress in Dublin (1932) was supported by a choir of five hundred voices, before an audience of one million. His rendition of Cesar Franck's *Panis Angelicus* was relayed into the streets of Dublin by loudspeaker, broadcast on radio and captured on film for the Pathe News.

Michael MacLiammoir (Alfred Lee Willmore), (1899-1978), Ardana, York Road, Dun Laoghaire; 57 Strand Road, Sandymount. Actor and founder, along with Hilton Edwards, of the Gate Theatre. Author of *All for Hecuba*, and *Ill Met By Moonlight*. Of the more Irish than the Irish themselves variety, having been born and reared in South London.

Eoin MacNeill, (1867-1954), lived at 3 and 4 South Hill Avenue, Booterstown. Patriot and academic. Helped to found the Gaelic League (1893). Professor of early Irish history at Trinity. Chief of Staff of the Irish Volunteers – issued the order countermanding the Easter Rising (1916). Later elected an MP for the National University of Ireland. Minister for Education in the first Free State government. Resigned following controversy over confirmation of borders with Northern Ireland. Dedicated later life to research.

Richard Madden, (1798-1886), lived at 4 Booterstown Avenue, and 3 Vernon Terrace, Booterstown. Author of the seven-volume *The United Irishmen - Their Lives and Times (1843-6)*. Employed in the civil service (1833-43), largely worked on the suppression of the slave trade in Jamaica, Havana and Africa. As Colonial Secretary for West Australia he tried to help the Aborigine people.

Flora Mitchell, (1890-1972), lived in Alloa, Killiney. An artist, her *Vanishing Dublin* is one of the most sought-after of the many books which have chronicled the city in recent decades.

Kevin O'Higgins, 1892-1927. Rented Lisaniskea (Lios an Uisce), Blackrock, from 1923 to 1925, later lived at Dunamase (St. Margaret's), Cross Avenue. Member of the Cabinet (Minister for Home Affairs – renamed Department of Justice in 1924) which authorised execution of prisoners during the Civil War. Closely involved with the development of the Garda Síochána. Assassinated on Cross Avenue while on his way to Mass in 1927. Winston Churchill described him as 'A figure out of the antique, cast in bronze.'

Brian O'Nolan (Flann O'Brien, Myles na gCopaleen), (1911-1966), 4 Avoca Road, Blackrock, 81 Mount Merrion Avenue. Irish Times columnist, novelist, punster ('Keats and Chapman') and civil servant (Department of Local Government and Public Health). *An Béal Bocht* (translated as *The Poor Mouth*) remains the only book in Irish I have ever willingly read – it's well worth the effort. He died, aptly, on All Fool's Day.

Sir William Orpen, (1878-1931), lived in Oriel, Grove Avenue, Blackrock. Painter – official war artist (1917-1919) in France (his war work can be seen at the Imperial War Museum, London). Possibly the most successful artist of his day he was an extremely fashionable portrait painter in the first two decades of the 20th century. Wrote two autobiographical works

An Outsider in France, 1917-1919 and *Stories of Old Ireland and Myself.* Has a permanent bay at the National Gallery of Ireland, Merrion Square, where his paintings of The Vere Foster Family; Noll Gogarty; The Dead Ptarmigan – a self-portrait, and The Artist's Parents can be seen.

Sir William Parsons, 3rd Earl of Rosse, (1800-1867), President of the Royal Society and Chancellor of the University of Dublin, died 1 Eaton Place, Monkstown. In 1845 he had erected the giant 72-inch Leviathan Telescope, then the largest in the world, in the grounds of Birr Castle, the family seat. The original mirror can still be seen at the Science Museum, London, while the telescope has been reconstructed at Birr Castle.

Richard Pigott, (1835-1889), 7 de Vesci Terrace, Monkstown. Publisher. Imprisoned several times for printing seditious material. In debt, he sold his publications, and began writing anonymous pamphlets. He forged a Charles Stuart Parnell letter which purported to show that the Irish leader was pleased by the murder of Burke, the Irish Under-Secretary by the Invincibles in the Phoenix Park (1892). It was printed by The Times (1897) and led to a Royal Commission. Pigott, asked to spell words which had been misspelled in the letter, broke down under cross-questioning. Fled to Madrid and committed suicide on March 1, 1889.

Dr. Joshua Pim, 1869-1942, 18 Crosthwaite Park, Dun Laoghaire, and 'Secrora', Killiney. Won the Wimbledon Doubles title (1890, 1893) and Singles title (1893, 1894). He was also Irish Singles Champion (1893-5) and, with Frank Stoker, Irish Doubles Champion (1890, 1891, 1893-5).

Sir Horace Plunkett, (1854-1932), lived at Kiltieragh, Foxrock (burnt down by Republicans in 1923). As a young man ranched for a decade in Wyoming. First President (1894) of the co-operative movement, the Irish Agricultural Organisation Society. Given credit for the establishment of the Department of Agriculture and Technical Instruction for Ireland (1899). Michael Collins was entertained at Kiltieragh, along with Lady Lavery and Bernard Shaw, three days before being shot dead in Cork.

James Henry Reynolds, 1844-1932, was born in Dun Laoghaire. Army surgeon who distinguished himself during the Battle of Rorke's Drift (1879). Under heavy fire, he both attended to the wounded and brought ammunition to the hospital defenders. Received one of 11 Victoria Crosses awarded to the defenders. A collection of items belonging to him, including a service revolver and field medical kit, was sold at Spinks, London, in 2001, for £36,000.

Lennox Robinson, (1886-1958), lived in Sorrento Cottage, Vico Road, Dalkey, (1925) and later at 20 Longford Terrace, Monkstown. Organising Librarian for Carnegie Trust (1915-24), dismissed after publication of his story *The Madonna of Slieve Dun*. Prolific playwright and Abbey Theatre manager. Plays include *The Clancy Name* and *The Whiteheaded Boy*. Wrote two autobiographical works *In Three Homes* and *Curtain Up*. Described by Micheál MacLiammoir as "long and boney as Don Quixote."

George Russell (AE), (1867-1935), lived at 5 Seapoint Terrace (1885-1898). Poet, painter and writer. Editor of the *Irish Homestead*, organ of the Irish Agricultural Organisation Society. Editor Irish Statesman (1923-1930). Friend of W. B. Yeats and Sir Horace Plunkett. Encouraged literary discussion but felt forced to leave Ireland after the Free State introduced severe censorship.

George Bernard Shaw (1856-1950). Spent youthful summers (1866-1874) at Torca Cottage, Dalkey, and attended a preparatory school at 23-24, Sandycove Road, Glasthule. Playwright, critic, political writer and curmudgeon. Awarded the Nobel Prize for Literature

(1925). He accepted the honour but refused the money. Best 1938 Screenplay Academy Award (Oscar) for *Pygmalion*.

"It's an insult," he railed. *"To offer me an award of this sort is an insult, as if they have never heard of me before … and it's very likely they never have."*

Works include *Man and Superman, Arms and the Man, John Bull's Other Island* and *Saint Joan*.

Annie M. P. Smithson, (1873-1948), born at 42 (then No. 22) Claremont Road, Sandymount, and, in her youth, lived on Barnhill Road, Dalkey. A district nurse - on the Republican side during the Civil War (she treated the wounded in Moran's Hotel during the attack, also in the Gresham and Hamman Hotels). Published 22 novels in 30 years. Popular works included *Her Irish Heritage, By Strange Paths, For God and Ireland* and *The Walk of a Queen*. Her autobiography, *Myself and Others*, was published in 1944.

James Stephens, (1824-1901), lived at 82 George's Avenue, Blackrock. Author and founder of the Fenians (IRB) and the Irish People newspaper (1863). Fell out with American Fenians after failing to organise a rising in 1865. Scratched a living in Paris until 1886 when money was raised to allow him to return home.

L. A. G. (Leonard Alfred George) Strong, (1896-1958), lived as a child at 37 Glasthule Road (demolished). Novelist, critic and man of letters. Encouraged while an undergraduate at Oxford by W. B. Yeats. Some of his novels have local interest, including *Sea Wall* (1933), concerning one Nicky D'Olier, which is set in Dun Laoghaire and Sandycove.

John Millington Synge, (1871-1909), lived at 31 Crosthwaite Park, Dun Laoghaire. Playwright. Advised by W. B. Yeats to write about life on the Aran Islands. His major play *The Playboy of the Western World* (1907) caused a week of riots at the Abbey - also caused trouble in Chicago, Boston and New York.

Captain Richard Toutcher, (1758-1841), successful agitator for the creation of a harbour in Dun Laoghaire. Lived for a time at Rumley Avenue (now Mulgrave Street).

Katherine Tynan (Hinkson), (1861-1931), lived in Cymric, Vico Road, and also, after her marriage in Kenah Hill, Killiney – the creation of Frank Dubedat. Author of more than 100 novels, also poetry and a five-volume autobiography. Her portrait, painted by John B. Yeats (1886) is in the Hugh Lane Gallery, Parnell Square. A close friend and confidant of his son, W. B. Yeats, she annoyed him by printing his letters to her without permission. Her daughter, Pamela Hinkson, (1900-1982), was also a writer.

Mervyn Wall, (1908-1997), novelist and playwright. Two of his novels are particularly funny – *The Unfortunate Fursey* and *The Return of Fursey*. He also wrote *Forty Foot Gentlemen Only*, a history of the famous Sandycove bathing place.

Maurice Walsh, (1879-1964), lived from 1933 in Ard na Glaise, Stillorgan Park Avenue, Blackrock, after retiring from the Civil Service. Moved in 1950 to Green Rushes in Avoca Road. Novelist (*The Quiet Man, Green Rushes, The Smart Fellow*) poet, detective and short story writer.

Peter Wilson, bookseller and publisher. Wrote his Topographical Letter from Dalkey Lodge in 1768.

Every morning and evening thousands of DART commuters pass by Booterstown Marsh – most hardly give it a glance. To many it's little more than a piece of bog transplanted into the suburbs – and it smells (not all the time, but enough!).

For city dwellers who can't tell a seagull from an eagle, there is little attraction in talk of Black-tailed Godwits, Redshank or Brent Geese. Others, however, take advantage of the surroundings to get close to nature without disturbing it. Their enjoyment is down to people like John Ducie, Vice Chairman of An Taisce (the Irish National Trust) who is also locally responsible for the Marsh.

Though not a bird fancier himself, he takes pride in the successes achieved since Booterstown Marsh was acquired on a lease from the Pembroke Estate in 1971.

"Dublin Bay is one of the top 14 wildlife areas in Europe," he says. *"Some of the world's most endangered migratory bird species spend their winters in Dublin Bay, and Booterstown is a very important part of that."*

An Taisce's involvement is not just a matter of organising annual clean-ups; the marsh has a mini-ecosystem which cannot be completely left to its own devices if both plants and birds are to flourish. A new automated sluice gate system is to be installed which An Taisce hopes will, over time, provide the right mix of salt and fresh water at different times.

"Habitats like this, particularly in an urban setting, have to be managed. We need, for example, to make it a slightly drier environment in the summer months to favour the protected Borrer's Saltmarsh-grass which is rare in Ireland," says John. *"By allowing more salt water in recent years – it increases oxygenation in the sediment – the number of birds arriving is at a ten-year high."*

Running costs are estimated at 30,000 Euro per year, An Taisce has a budget of just 2,000 Euro. *"Everything is done by voluntary effort,"* notes John. *"We're one of just four European countries without legislation to provide a framework for a voluntary National Trust. As a result we struggle."*

Booterstown Marsh

Of the history of Booterstown (Baile an Bhóthar - the town of the road) we know little before the coming of the Normans – though the Slighe Cualan, one of the five great roads of ancient Ireland, ran through the area.

The first Norman owner was Walter de Ridelsford (1173). His granddaughter, Christiana, eventually exchanged her estate at Booterstown for land in England. A later owner was William Fitzwilliam who, in 1348, was given a pardon for any crime he may have committed while fighting the Irish.

Thomas Fitzwilliam was knighted (1566) for his exploits against Shane O'Neill and some say he was bribed to help Hugh O'Donnell and his companions escape from Dublin Castle. The Fitzwilliams eventually moved to England and Merrion Castle was taken down in the mid-19th century.

In 1826 the Rev. George Wogan, for 26 years a curate at St. Mary's, Donnybrook, was murdered during a robbery at his home at Spafield Place. A servant, Kelly, who was beaten, was initially suspected but Michael Hynes and George Stanley of Grotto Place, arrested for a highway robbery the same night on Blackrock Road, confessed during their trial.

The events of July 10, 1927, rocked Ireland. Kevin O'Higgins, Vice-President of the Government, became the first, and so far, only, Minister to be assassinated. No one was ever tried but decades later the killers were identified as IRA members, however their motives remain unclear. Most likely it was the bitter residue of the Civil War in which O'Higgins had played a leading part, defending the executions of 77 Republicans - including that of Rory O'Connor who, a year before, had been best man at his wedding.

That Sunday morning O'Higgins left his home, Dunamase, in Cross Avenue, and walked alone towards Booterstown Church. On Booterstown Avenue three gunmen (now known to have been Archie Doyle, Tim Murphy and Bill Gannon) opened fire and O'Higgins, after staggering a few steps, fell to the ground. The gunmen continued firing, and then escaped in a car.

O'Higgins, though mortally wounded, lasted another five hours, during which he repeatedly forgave his killers. He was just 35.

Booterstown
– the town of the road

The 'Circus Field' in Booterstown has, according to circus folk, the distinction of being the only official local authority site in the country, north and south.

They say that 20 years ago, Dun Laoghaire Borough Corporation councillors voted to give the site the status to mark the enjoyment the circus had brought to generations.

But 20 years is a long time in politics and the building of a halting site for Travellers and the provision of a cycle track have both eaten into the space available. A report prepared recently for Dun Laoghaire Rathdown County Council argued that the remaining space was no longer sufficient for circus use. Councillors decided to ignore that report and again voted for its continued use by circuses.

But other problems continue to cause difficulty, including the lack of parking in the immediate area and a limit of between 10 and 20 posters in Dun Laoghaire Rathdown. Dublin Corporation, whose boundary lies just down the road, has a much more relaxed approach to postering. On the bright side is the introduction of a new Art Bill by the government, which recognises circus as an art form. This, circuses hope, places a responsibility on local authorities to provide resources for them.

The two circuses most closely linked to the site are Duffy's (Ireland's Premier Circus) and Fossett's (Ireland's National Circus). Duffy's can normally be found in Booterstown in June or July, while Fossett's arrives in October.

Today's circus is, according to Charles O'Brien of Fossett's, much bigger and faster paced than decades ago.

"The big tent now holds 750 people, it used to be just 300. The show is influenced by TV, 20 years ago the circus had a slower pace, today it has to be immediate. We have massive lighting rigs and powerful sound systems because that's what people want."

"But the atmosphere is probably the same. People like the circus to be on grass, they want the smells and even like to hear the rain banging on the tent while they're enjoying themselves. The core acts remain the same but the presentation has been brought right up to date."

The Circus Field

When Père Leman (1826-1880) of the Holy Ghost Fathers (subsequently known locally as the 'French Fathers') arrived in Ireland in 1859 his plan was to recruit missionaries for Africa. The response was disappointing and he noticed that the educational standard of those who had shown an interest was not particularly good.

He became convinced that only by educating boys from an early age would suitable missionary candidates become available. It was a belief which was only reluctantly shared by the Congregation of the Holy Ghost, but permission was finally given for the foundation of a college.

In 1860 Castle Dawson at Williamstown, between Booterstown and Blackrock, was acquired. Three further substantial properties (Williamstown Castle, Clareville, [later demolished], and Willow Park) were added between then and 1924 to create the present college and grounds. The growth of the college led to the demolition of many smaller houses on the west side of the Rock Road. New houses were erected at Emmet Square in 1908 to house some of the families affected.

Rugby is the main sport for which the college is known at home and internationally. Many Blackrock players have gone on to win International Caps, from Patrick Joseph O'Connor in 1887 to Neil Francis, Fergus Slattery and Brian O'Driscoll.

The school also excels at other sports. The Willow Park Wheelers, founded in 1989, now has over 100 members who take part in 40km to 100km cycles on Sundays. An annual charity cycle is held to raise funds for the Holy Ghost Fathers' mission in Sierra Leone.

Over 1,000 pupils now attend Blackrock College, which is recognised as one of the premier schools in Dublin. Not surprisingly there have been many famous alumni most notably the man who shaped the Irish state after 1921, Eamon de Valera. John Charles McQuaid, Archbishop of Dublin (1940-1972), studied at Blackrock College, as did one of the founders of the Legion of Mary, Frank Duff.

One former student of whom Père Leman would be proud is Bob Geldof, organiser of the Live Aid Concert and constant supporter of, and fundraiser for, the Third World.

Blackrock College

The decision to construct two piers at Dun Laoghaire meant that the original asylum harbour had become a full blown trading port – a fast connection to Dublin became a priority. A ship canal was considered too expensive and the daring suggestion surfaced that maybe a railway could be built.

First it was necessary to judge what traffic already existed. Clerks, stationed in Blackrock, from February to October 1831, 6 a.m. to 9 p.m. each day, counted: 29,256 Private Carriages, 113,495 Private Jaunting Cars, 149,754 Public Cars, and many other forms of transport.

Railway was in its infancy and certainly still unproven on this scale in Ireland. The idea also met with substantial opposition from landowners along the proposed line from Westland Row to Dun Laoghaire. Even today the line shows the evidence of what transpired – a tunnel, bridges, towers and private bathing places were provided at substantial cost.

William Dargan agreed to build everything except the stations and other buildings, engines and coaches, for £84,000. The first sod was turned on April 11, 1833. Stone was brought from Seapoint cliffs and Dalkey, nearer to Dublin, Donnybrook limestone was used.

Work near Merrion proved difficult as the land was below the high-water level and drainage proved difficult.

From there to Blackrock it was necessary to build embankments, reclaiming about 50 acres from the sea.

The first train (drawn by horses) carried the company directors and their friends over the line on July 31, 1834. On October 4, the engine 'Vauxhall' brought a short train from Westland Row to Williamstown and back. Within days there were trips to Dun Laoghaire, and on December 18 the line opened. The terminus was then at the West Pier. There were nine further trips that day *all packed to discomfort"* (DART users please note) and *"applauded by crowds."*

On the hour there were trains from both ends of the line from 9 a.m. to 4 p.m. An extension of the line, began in 1836, destroyed the original Dún (an earthwork) from which Dun Laoghaire takes it name, and the Martello Tower inside it. It also created what is now the main railway station (Mallin Station) beside the entrance to the Harbour.

The Coming of the Railway

Blackrock (Newtown-on-the-Strand, or Newtown-at-the-Black-Rock) is named after the large black rock which could once be seen ofrf-shore.

That rock in medieval times marked the edge of the area controlled by the city of Dublin and the Mayor of Dublin, on his regular check of the boundary, stopped briefly there before moving inland.

By the end of the reign of George II (1683-1760) the town had become a fashionable resort and an early map (1802) shows Blackrock Town with Baths for Men, separated by the Black Rock from the Baths for Women.

Not everyone was in high spirits, in 1754 Sir Charles Moore went missing after going for a dip at the Black Rock. He was later found, fully-clothed, shot dead. He'd been thoughtful enough to bring a second loaded pistol with him, though one proved sufficient! A jury considered the case for two days before returning the verdict 'lunatick.'

Over the years Blackrock has had its share of substantial buildings. Some survive though others have been demolished, most notably Frescati (the site of the house is now a car park).

Frescati, though not the permanent home of Lord Edward Fitzgerald (leader of the 1798 Rebellion), was very dear to him. In a letter to his mother he wrote:

'Wife and I come to settle here. We came last night, got up to a delightful spring day ... I am sitting in the bay window with all those pleasant feelings which the fine weather, the pretty place, the singing birds, the pretty wife, and Frescati give me.'

The coming of the railway did Blackrock few favours as it created a 'malodorous swamp', and cut off access to the shore.

By the 1850's Blackrock had its own Urban District Council, which also included Booterstown and Monkstown, and the foundation stone of the Town Hall (now a library and education centre currently being restored) was laid on February 15, 1865. Eight years later the Town Commissioners filled in the 'malodorous swamp' to create Blackrock Park.

At Blackrock can be found the oddest by-pass in Dublin with no fewer than seven sets of traffic lights within a few hundred yards. When it was being built motorists were told they could take advantage of the 'Green Wave', instead they encounter the 'Red Crawl.'

Blackrock

In times gone by the facilities for entertainment were fewer than today – no cinema, radio or television. People had to make do with what was available, and what was available from earliest times, was the pub or tavern.

Among the older pubs in our area are The Purty Kitchen (known as the Dunleary Inn in 1728), The Punch Bowl, Booterstown (1742) and The Queens', Dalkey, (which was established in 1745 as The Red Crowe).

But, enough of history, people don't choose to spend their time in pubs because they're historic. Here's a light-hearted introduction to what you can expect to find in our public houses.

THE OLD PUB.

Old pubs can often be identified from their modesty screen, which prevents all but the tallest from viewing life within. The interior is kept perpetually dim in keeping with the principle that bright light should be only used when a publican really has to get people off the premises. If you want to see the outside world you only have to walk out the door. A common complaint from those departing is that reality is excessively bright.

The exterior is often Victorian or Edwardian and normally bears the name of the proprietor, a local landmark or event. The interior can range from exquisitely carved wood fittings to formica, but wood, copper and brass are the norm.

Old pubs have only a small radio to keep in touch with the outside world, and then only for important sporting occasions. Some may have a television set – it, too, only serves as a connection to the world of sport. Occasional exceptions are made, but, like background music, the always-on TV is considered heretical.

Only on very special occasions is singing allowed – bringing both your great-grandparents in almost qualifies. By common consent the discussion of politics and religion is considered unhelpful. Those preparing to fight are normally advised to "Take it outside!"

Dietary requirements are taken care of by offering crisps and salted peanuts. More advanced old pubs may offer a sandwich (sometimes toasted) but never anything involving lettuce.

Prices are almost invariably pegged at the same level as other nearby pubs, a method of competition which ensures that the regular customer doesn't get confused.

Pubs
- What's Yours

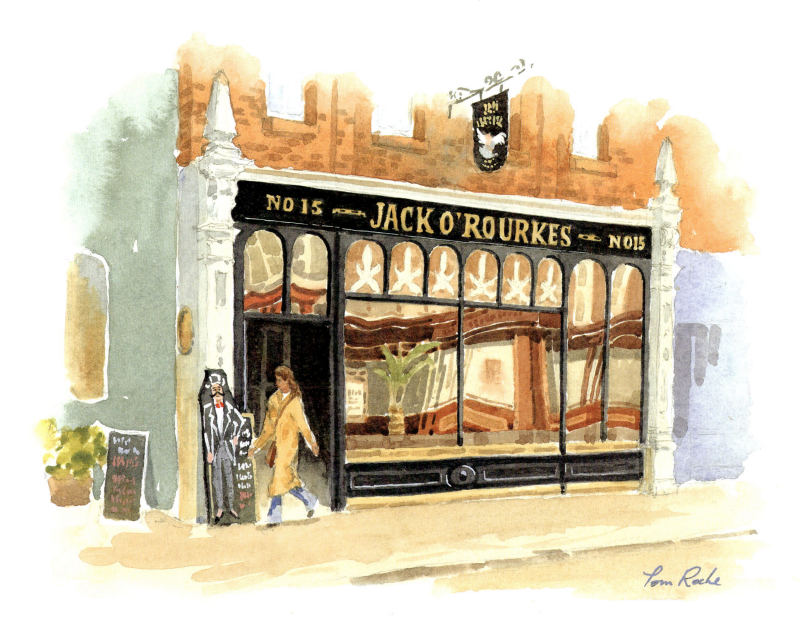

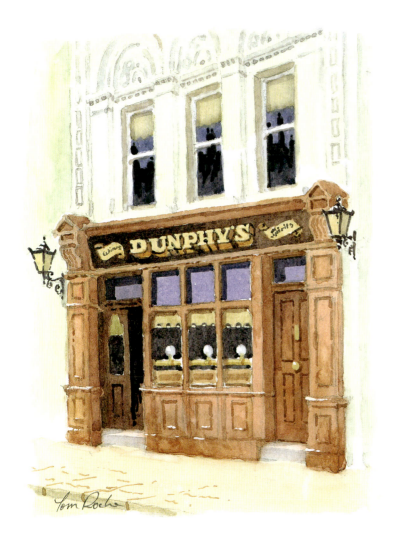

THE NEW PUB

The new pub believes in showing what it's got, brazenly revealing to the outside world that people are drinking alcohol in brightly lit conditions. Premises such as these usually serve more types of coffee than beer, and offer a bewildering array of 'by the neck' drinks in shades of blue, yellow and red.

The menu offers a selection of exotic food from many lands and various items of tasteful pub memorabilia (t-shirts, golf umbrellas and the like) are on sale.

The television constantly shows MTV but the music comes from a pre-prepared tape. Singing is not prohibited but is simply made impossible by the din.

The exterior can resemble anything from a DIY store to a church but rarely a pub. Interior design varies wildly though a steel and marble finish is common. The name above the door can be a squiggle, a concept or just a number.

Religion and politics are rarely discussed, but only because the goings-on of TV reality show contestants is considered far more interesting.

Prices are competitive, i.e. the operators compete to find somewhere within 20 miles that charges more and then adjust their price upwards.

The concept of a price war is considered dangerous –
any lowering of prices is considered by vintners to be as
bizarre a concept as an investigation of why soft drinks,
which have no excise duty, are more expensive than
alcoholic ones.

THE REAL PUB.

The Real Pub is the one you're stuck with. While our
towns have many pubs, most suburban dormitory areas
have only one or two and some areas have none within
easy walking distance.

This pub is distinguished by customers who probably
would prefer to be somewhere else, but somewhere else is
too far away.

During the summer months rare novelty is provided by
groups of Spanish students who are in Ireland to brush up
on their English. They rarely drink, the gradual lowering
of their single potion being somewhat akin to osmosis.

It has a golf society and some kind of weekly draw is
normally held. Regular 21st birthday parties, Golden
Wedding celebrations, Pub Quizzes and Discos are held.

It is at the forefront of objections to any new licensed
premises in the area – one pub is enough for any area, a
view shared by residents who, having accepted the
occasional annoyance caused by one pub have no wish to
experiment with a second.

Monkstown and Monkstown Farm are the two areas locally whose names stem from their history as possessions of St. Mary's Abbey. Until the Reformation the abbey, which stood off present-day Capel Street in central Dublin, was the largest landowner south of the Liffey. After that time there were new owners (see 'Carrickbrennan') but for centuries Monkstown remained rural as shown by its inclusion in the song *The Kilruddery Hunt* which remembers an exciting chase in winter 1744.

"He drove on by Bullock, through Shrub Glenageary,
And so on to Monkstown where Larry grew weary."

Rocque's map (1757) shows open countryside at Monkstown with the Dunlary Road (Monkstown Road) passing through. During the United Irishmen's rebellion in 1798 most of the residents of Monkstown and Blackrock went before a judge and declared themselves loyal.

As late as the 1830s Monkstown was described as '*a locality not perhaps in itself either town or village, but surrounded by elegant villas, noble demesnes, and tasteful bathing lodges.*' The same writer, Dalton, noted that Monkstown had two schools attended by 295 pupils, a hospital (with four wards of eight beds) and a dispensary.

The hospital expanded in 1880 and remained open until 1988.

We're so used to Monkstown Parish Church in the centre of village that we rarely give it a second glance. But, when it was built and for long after, it was often criticised. F. E. Ball described it as a '*grotesque structure.*' Weston St. John Joyce gave it the thumbs down as a '*nondescript structure which disfigures its site,*' but for real venom Dr. Richard Brooke, its first incumbent, can't be beaten: '*Large and gaunt, and lofty and ugly – a satire on taste, a libel on all ecclesiastical rule, mocking at proportion and symmetry.*'

Opened in 1832, replacing one built between 1785 and 1789 because more space was needed, it was built at the start of the population explosion in the area. Work began on St. Patrick's Roman Catholic Church in 1861 and was completed five years later. Though further back from central Monkstown it is also an impressive structure.

Today the area of Monkstown, once the extensive hub of south Dublin, has contracted to little more than a square mile. It is best known to Dubliners for its many restaurants, mainly centred on Monkstown Crescent, the Lambert Puppet Theatre, and fine houses from many periods.

Monkstown

Close to Monkstown Castle lies Carrickbrennan cemetery and the remains of a 9th century church. It was from early times the property of the Abbey of St. Mary in Dublin.

After the Reformation Carrickbrennan was disused for over 100 years. The church was rebuilt and used as Monkstown Church of Ireland Church (1668 to 1789) until the increasing Protestant population moved to the newly built Monkstown Parish Church nearby.

In the early 19th century the cemetery church became a watchman's hut to prevent body snatchers from carrying out their ghoulish trade. The double wall was built to make the theft of the dead more difficult.

The cemetery contains memorials to the *Rochdale* and *Prince of Wales*. Both troopships foundered on November 19, 1807 in atrocious weather. *The Prince of Wales* was driven onto the rocks in Blackrock and 120 died after Captain Jones took his crew off in the only lifeboat. The Rochdale went aground in pitch darkness near the Seapoint Martello Tower. All 194 soldiers, 42 women and 29 children on board died. When morning came it was found that the stricken ship was only 12 feet from shore.

Another memorial is to the crew of the coastguard vessel *Ajax* who died on February 9, 1861. During a blizzard the *Ajax* launched a boat to aid the *Neptune*, which had run aground behind the East Pier in Dun Laoghaire, just 20 feet from shore. Captain John MacNeil Boyd and his crew were swept away. Six of the seven *Neptune* crew also died.

In Carrickbrennan can also be found the grave of 1798 Insurgent leader Joseph Holt (1756-1826). The son of a wealthy farmer he was an unlikely rebel. Denounced by his landlord as a United Irishman, his home was destroyed by the yeomanry, an experience that gave him common cause with the rebels. As luck would have it Joseph Holt turned out to be an excellent leader and rose rapidly to high command. Eventually, by a settlement brokered through his wife, he was transported as a free man to Australia. He returned to Ireland in April 1814 and opened a pub in Kevin Street but it was not successful and he retired to Dun Laoghaire.

Unfortunately access to the cemetery is now restricted.

Carrickbrennan Graveyard

The early history of Monkstown Castle is unclear though we know that it was built by the monks of St. Mary's Abbey in the 13th or 14th century to protect their holdings. The area of Carrickbrennan, and much more besides, had been granted to the Abbey by Henry II in 1174.

From various reports we know that what remains of the castle today is but a fraction of a much more impressive structure in which a mansion house, with six chimneys, stood in a large courtyard guarded by three large towers. The large courtyard (a bawn) was used to temporarily house sheep, cattle and tenants whenever there was danger of attack. The monks themselves farmed some of the surrounding land and let other portions to tenants.

A report at the end of the 13th century described Monkstown as worthless because it was constantly being raided by various warring factions. A few years later the monks had to negotiate with the Irish tribes and pay a 'Black Rent' for the return of some of their property.

Control of the area passed out of their hands in 1539, as part of the Dissolution of the Monasteries, when it was given by Henry VIII to Sir John Travers, a military adventurer.

After the 1641 Rebellion the owner, Walter Cheevers, was deported, along with his family, servants and some livestock to Connaught. The castle was granted by Oliver Cromwell to General Edmund Ludlow, one of the regicides of King Charles I.

A 1654 survey noted the townland of Monkstown contained an old castle, newly repaired, also a mill in use, a small creek, a parish church in repair, and a small shrubby wood with a few ash trees. With the restoration of Charles II in 1660 the castle was returned to the Cheevers family. Later it was owned by Michael Boyle, Archbishop of Armagh. Through the marriage of his daughters it came into the joint ownership of the Longford and De Vesci families.

By 1789 the castle went up for sale again and was described as '*the second best ... on the south side of the Liffey.*' But 50 years later the castle had fallen into disrepair – it's not clear why.

Monkstown Castle

There's never been a shortage of artists living along the south Dublin coastline. But as the country built up its infrastructure after Independence, their work was largely ignored – at least as far as the local authorities were concerned.

One of those who felt that a little artistic colour could be applied in public was Cllr. Jane Dillon-Byrne, herself a sculptor and artist. She, and others, organised a sculpture symposium locally in 1987.

A list of sites was prepared and sculptors were invited along to take a bus trip and come up with ideas for pieces which might be suitable. When the entries were whittled down, the then College of Art provided studio space, while the local authority provided board and keep and a small annuity for the sculptors while they worked.

"I think it was successful, it opened people's eyes to a new type of visual experience, they were durable and of a very high standard," says Cllr. Dillon-Byrne. *"There was criticism that some works were not suitable for the area they ended up in, but most blended in quite well."*

Some years later, the government introduced a one per cent levy on capital developments for art. This allowed local authorities to commission larger pieces in areas being developed. Among those which have been funded by the levy are the *Blackrock Dolmen,* as part of the Blackrock Bypass, and *Mothership*, commissioned under the Dun Laoghaire Drainage Scheme.

More recently, according to Cllr. Dillon-Byrne, there seems to be little enthusiasm for the provision of public art. *"Nothing was put in the George's Street development. There is also a move towards funding local arts initiatives which do not involve sculpture."* She remains hopeful, however, that some of the upcoming major developments will be of artistic interest. *"We cannot exclude architecture from art and I believe there are great opportunities in the development of the Carlisle Pier, Dun Laoghaire and Blackrock Baths sites."*

Opp. L to R
1) Old Dalkey Head by Tom Glendon. Swan's Hollow, Glenageary. Ballyknockan Granite. (1986)
2) Mothership by Rachel Joynt, Newtownsmith, Sandycove. 2m. Castle Bronze and Stainless Steel. (1999).
3) The Blackrock Dolmen by Rowan Gillespie. Blackrock Bypass. Bronze and Resin Bronze. (1997)

Public Sculpture

The middle of a housing estate is not where you would expect to find an ancient ruined abbey but such is the case with Kill-o'the-Grange or Kill Abbey. In the past 70 years the suburbs have swept through and the ruined church, now walled in to protect against vandalism, stands surrounded.

In ancient times the area was called Cluinchenn (Clonkeen), later as Kill-o'the-Grange (the Abbey of St. Mary had a farm or grange here), and Dean's Grange after the Reformation. It was dedicated to St. Fintain and continued in use until the time of Cromwell.

Today, people like Sally and Sean Farrelly, Joseph Byrne and Fran Doyle remember when the old church stood in semi-rural isolation, when cross-country runs could be taken for miles without manmade obstacle, when Sunday evening handball matches at the Garda station alley drew crowds, the surrounding area had nurseries and orchards and it was not considered unusual to visit seven churches on Holy Thursday.

They recall a time when TB was a constant threat and the Lourdes Hospital catered for TB victims from all over; when Clonkeen Road, overhung by branches and only dimly lit by the moon, was a favoured location for courting; when Silkes (now much enlarged as Bakers Corner) was the local pub, George Dowdall ran the local shop selling newspapers and sweets, and Lar Breen, with his two cows, had 300 customers (presumably people didn't drink much milk then).

They remember when the Dun Laoghaire Institute of Art, Design and Technology was the Carriglea Industrial School, teaching shoemaking, carpentry and tailoring, and the young 'inmates' were only ever brought walking out under supervision. The threat of being sent to Carriglea was enough to soften the cough of even the most unruly local child.

One treasured memory concerns the time a fight was arranged outside the Garda Station and a car found it impossible to get through. The lady driver approached the Sergeant, leaning out the window and ensuring the Queensbury Rules weren't completely ignored, and asked him to put an end to it. *"Madam,"* he replied, *"You can blame de Valera, there are too many problems around and they just need to get it out of their systems!"*

What would the monks of Kill Abbey have made of it all?

Kill Abbey

Life in Victorian Dun Laoghaire could be very harsh. Families were often large and it was not unusual if the breadwinner fell ill or died for the family to experience a headlong descent into poverty.

In 1879 an Englishwoman, Rosa Parkes, set up a day nursery for Protestant children under five, in a cottage on York Road. The service was soon extended to include some resident children. Whenever possible, parents were expected to pay towards the cost, but, in reality, the Home was run by voluntary subscription and fundraising. As numbers grew the need for a larger, purpose-built premises became evident. A site was found on the Tivoli Road frontage of Royal Terrace and the architect W. Kaye Parry, drew up the plans free of charge.

The Cottage Home for Little Children opened on December 17, 1887. Seventeen children, all dressed in new clothes, marched to their new home. Numbers continued to grow and it was normal to find 40 or 50 children there.

In 1894 one of the trustees of the home, Thomas P. Cairnes, died and his widow decided to fund, in his memory, an extension to the building. The extension, adding three bedrooms and two sitting rooms, completed the building as we know it today.

Conditions at the home were good and the statistics show that, while the average mortality of children under five in Dublin city was 81.5 per 1,000, there were 10 deaths per thousand children there. In fact, from 1901 to early January 1915, no deaths occurred.

Down through the years Rosa Barrett had been a constant presence but in 1920 she retired in ill health to England, though remaining a member of the Committee and acting President until her death in 1936.

Adoption became legal in Ireland in 1953 and the numbers of children at the Cottage Home began to fall slowly but steadily. In the 1980s the Cottage Home increased the age limit from under-fives to about 16. Today there are two satellite houses, one in Dun Laoghaire, the other in Ballinteer, where children live in conditions as close as possible to that of a family home.

The original building is the administration centre as well as providing short-term accommodation for a few children and, as was originally intended, day care.

Adapted with permission from *One Hundred Years A-Growing – 1879-1979* by Olive C. Goodbody and *The Cottage Home*, by Rob Goodbody, Dun Laoghaire Journal No. 11, 2002.

The Cottage Home for Little Children

What links the one-time richest man in the world with Dun Laoghaire? – The answer is, of course, Dun Laoghaire Public Library!

It, and over 2,800 libraries around the world, were provided at the expense of Andrew Carnegie (1835-1919), Scottish-born American immigrant, self-made man and the 'King of Steel.'

In 1901 he sold out to J. P. Morgan and received $450 million, which he promptly spent the rest of his life giving away. Typically, he paid for the building of a library, basing the amount given on the local population. In return the local authority had to agree to its upkeep.

The Dun Laoghaire Carnegie Library was built in 1912. It contains a specialist local history section which has directories from 1798 and newspapers from 1819. Rare books include Grose's *Antiquities of Ireland* (1791), and Warburton's *History of the City of Dublin* (1818).

The premises which until recently housed the Workmen's Club is next door to the Carnegie Library. Founded close to the Coal Quay by Prof. William. F. Barrett in 1893, it offered newspapers and books, draughts and skittles, but no alcohol was allowed. Tobacco was sold – a penny to fill a large pipe – and a yearly highlight was the Annual Smoking Concert. Workmen were also offered, for three pence, a hot bath – with soap and towel thrown in.

The club moved to Lower George's Street in 1915. There were regular dances and there was a summer outing each year.

In 1958 the Workmen's Club took a 200-year lease on a five-acre site on Rochestown Avenue for use as a football ground. The Club had been fielding soccer teams from 1905 – including Dunleary United (the Blues). Members also took part in boxing, athletics and rowing.

A slow decline in membership led to the decision to wind up the Workmen's Club and, in 2002 the building was sold for 1.6 million Euro. A planning application was lodged for retail and office use. What will happen to the football grounds is unclear.

Carnegie Library and the Workmen's Club

CARNEGIE LIBRARY
1912

Tom Roche

A year after the end of WWI a simple Oratory was built in the grounds of the Dominican Sisters (now Bloomfields Shopping Centre) to house a statue of the Sacred Heart, which had been sent from Flanders to remember the men from Dun Laoghaire, who died in France.

By happy coincidence one of the nuns, Sister Mary Concepta Lynch, O.P., (1874-1936), had been trained as a 'Celtic' artist before she entered religious life at the age of 22. Between 1920 and 1936, when ill health forced her to leave the work unfinished, she used her talent to turn the bare interior into a celebration of the 'Celtic' style of art. This style, which originated in the mid 19th century, relied heavily on the work of the monastic scribes, the Books of Kells and Durrow, the Ardagh Chalice and other Irish treasures.

By the time Sr. Concepta began her work, the movement had begun to experiment and to incorporate elements of modern art, including Art Deco and Art Nouveau. Her work, however, remains firmly within the traditional mode, and was planned as an integrated whole rather than a series of unconnected pieces. Her designs are also used on the seven stained-glass windows by Harry Clarke.

She worked by drawing her designs on paper which she then used as stencils. When carefully examined it becomes obvious that many of the basic designs have been duplicated many times. When the design was mapped out Sr. Concepta then used free-hand brushwork, in warm colours, to complete the fine details.

In 1958, another nun, Sister M. Theodora, O.P., completed work on the plain floor. Her design, based on the back of the Shrine of St. Patrick's Bell (12th century), has a series of dark wooden crosses outlined against a lighter parquet background.

Oratory of the Sacred Heart

At the very centre of Dun Laoghaire is George's Street Lower and Upper - the former section, from Marine Road (St. Michael's Church) to Library Road having been singled out for improvement recently.

Footpaths have been widened and cars banned. Cobblestones were laid to encourage traffic to slow down and not, as some wags have suggested, to provide a regular supply of broken limbs to nearby St. Michael's Hospital.

It was from George's Street that the town of Dun Laoghaire grew – an old map showing it calls Dun Leary 'Old Town' and George's Street the 'New Town.' What had been barren land provided plenty of opportunities for building and soon other streets grew from it.

Although none of the Victorian shopfronts seen in old photographs have endured, many buildings show interesting features on the uppers storeys and there are other echoes of years gone by.

Vera Breslin is one of the most familiar faces in Dun Laoghaire. Every Wednesday, Thursday and Friday she can be found at her fishmonger's stall at the junction of Lower George's Street with Convent Road.

Her family have been selling fish locally for many generations, no-one is quite sure just how far back that goes. What is certain is that Vera has been selling fish at several different locations in the centre of Dun Laoghaire since she joined her mother on the stall at just seven years of age.

She intends to continue for as long as her health allows - she's in excellent health!

"It's nice here," Vera says. *"I have a chat with my regular customers, some of them come up from Bray, and the local shop assistants are very nice, every one of them!"*

Central
Dun Laoghaire

B uilt to link the town with the harbour, Marine Road is now often criticised because it has come to symbolise the separation of the two.

It was not ever so. Until it burnt down in 1915 the highly ornamental Pavilion Gardens (where the new Pavilion Centre now stands) provided every form of entertainment; concerts, talks, food and drink, fine views of the harbour and, of course, a decorative garden.

When it was rebuilt it had lost much of its architectural quality and, having burnt down again, eventually became a featureless concrete block which, according to local historian and author Peter Pearson, was *"the first blot on Dun Laoghaire's Victorian image."*

It continued in use as a popular cinema and concert hall until the mid-70s after which time it was allowed to decay into a major eyesore before being demolished.

Across the road can be seen the new County Hall which incorporates the old Post Office (1879-1995) and the Town Hall (1878), both of which were designed by J. L. Robinson.

Until recently the Gresham Royal Marine Hotel could be easily seen just off Marine Road, but it is now mostly obscured by a large apartment building while at the George's Street end of Marine Road is the rather ugly – functional if you prefer – shopping centre which dates from the 1970s.

St. Michael's Church, was another victim of fire and all that remains of the original structure (1920-1965) is the tower and spire (now housing the Youth Information Centre).

Marine Road

The Victoria Fountain, at the entrance to Dun Laoghaire Harbour, was erected in 1901 to commemorate the visit to Dun Laoghaire of Queen Victoria the year before. It was vandalised in 1981 and what remained was removed to storage. The restored monument incorporates some of the original features including the fountain itself, the granite base and two cast iron lamp standards.

Public opinion is divided over it. Some people see it as a fine example of decorative ironwork; others can take it or leave it. There is also a body of opinion that it is in the worst possible bad taste to recreate in 2003 a 1901 monument to the 'Famine Queen,' and, of course, there are many who wish we would just grow up and stop whining about the past.

The Harbour Company has dedicated the public space around what they refer to as the Victorian Fountain to the memory of the workmen who built the Harbour. There was no official re-dedication of the fountain. Sinn Fein issued a statement at the dedication of the public space: *Where else in the world would you get a country that gained its independence through conflict and struggle erecting monuments to their former colonial masters?"*

But it cannot be denied that there is a clear link between Queen Victoria and the harbour. She passed through the harbour on several occasions (1849, 1853, 1861 and, finally, in 1900). And it is fair to say that these were exciting and busy days in the life of the area.

An excerpt from her diary, Viceregal Lodge, Phoenix Park, Monday, August 6, 1849, reads:

"We steamed slowly and majestically into the harbour of Kingstown, which was covered with thousands and thousands of spectators, cheering most enthusiastically. It is a splendid harbour, and was full of ships of every kind.

As the clock struck ten we disembarked, stepping on shore from the yacht, Albert leading me and the children, and all the others following us. An immense multitude had assembled, who cheered most enthusiastically, the ships saluting and the bands playing, and it was really most striking. The space we had to walk along to the railroad was covered in; and lined with ladies and gentlemen strewing flowers."

Victoria Fountain

John Rocque's map of 1756 clearly shows the small fishing village and harbour of Dunlary from which, less than half a century later, was to spring the new town of Dun Laoghaire.

The origin of the name is obscure though there is no doubt that it was linked to an earthwork fort (a dún) which stood near the coal harbour approximately at the junction of Clarence Street and Crofton Road.

Who was Laoghaire or Leary? There are two theories put forward. The first theory is that Laoghaire was an unknown person who lived up to 2,000 years ago. He built a fort here to protect the natural harbour. The second is that Laoghaire was high king of Ireland at the time when St. Patrick arrived (432). Above the harbour he built a large fort. Whether either is true will never be known. The fort was completely destroyed when the railway was being built.

Rocque's map was published just as work began on improving the old harbour to give shelter to ships in times of bad weather. By 1761 the Trustees of the Harbour reported that many ships had been saved, including *The Hare* of Dublin, from New York with lumber, and the *Skerries Barge*, laden with seized teas, brandy, and tobacco.

A visitor, Austin Cooper, described the old harbour as a handsome, semi-circular structure, enclosed by high banks of gravel, and by the pier, which was about 27 perches (about 140m) long, which sheltered it from all winds except the north.

Silting, however, was a problem which was never overcome.

With the building of the new harbour, Old Dunleary was swiftly eclipsed by Dun Laoghaire. Today the row of houses, which include the Purty Kitchen, is all that remains to remind us of the village that once was.

Old Dunleary

Over one million people live in the greater Dublin area and it is estimated that every year about half of them take advantage of one of our great natural assets, Dublin Bay.

However, the growth of the city meant that the practice of dumping sewage into the Bay had long been a problem – in *Ulysses*, James Joyce recalls an infamous case of food poisoning: *'Poor man O'Connor wife and five children poisoned by mussels here. The sewage.'*

It was a situation which could not be allowed to last, particularly as the European Union began to insist on proper sewage management and protection of the environment. The introduction of the Blue Flag scheme also highlighted shortcomings in the maintenance of the bay and shoreline.

As part of the 300 million Euro Dublin Bay Project, waste water from most of Dublin is pumped to Ringsend Treatment Works for totally natural processing using oxygen, steam and heat. The 20,000 tonnes of organic, pasteurised fertiliser which is produced, is sold and spread on tillage land in Leinster. The gas produced provides half of the annual energy needs of the plant.

The completion of the Dublin Bay Project in 2003 brings both Merrion and Sandymount Strands to European Water Standards for the first time.

The West Pier Pumping Station, which sends local waste water to Ringsend, was built as part of the Dun Laoghaire Drainage Scheme between 1989 and 1991 at a cost of 8.9 million Euro.

Special attention was paid by architects P. H. McCarthy and Partners to the exterior of the Pumping Station as it occupies a visibly sensitive site. The three blocks are clad in Wicklow granite and have flared pyramidal roofs covered in black slate. The interior contains several large murals. The Pumping Station is not normally open to the public.

Seapoint has recently regained its Blue Flag status and is the only Dublin beach this year (2003) to have been awarded one. Others beaches are expected to gain this award in the near future.

The Pumping Station, West Pier

The creation of Dun Laoghaire Harbour came about by accident – those of the *Rochdale* and the *Prince of Wales* in November 1807. Until then, although there were problems with the port of Dublin, planning had concentrated on improving conditions there through dredging and the building of the North and South Bull Walls.

It was thought the problem had already been partly addressed, with the decision in 1807 to proceed with the building of a large port at Howth. This proved unsuitable as its harbour mouth was subject to silting. One factor, which mitigated against selecting the existing harbour at Dun Laoghaire, was that it had been greatly extended and improved just 50 years before at a cost of £18,500 (£2,500 under-budget!).

In 1807, as Dublin prepared to bury some 400 troops, sailors and civilians from the *Rochdale* and *Prince of Wales* disasters, the debate on preventing such disasters in the future reached fever pitch. Richard Toutcher, a seaman and ship owner, called a meeting in Monkstown to discuss the provision of an asylum harbour. Only a few hundred yards away from the existing and unsuitable Dun Laoghaire harbour, he argued, there was sufficient deep water to build an asylum harbour and give guaranteed safety.

Toutcher kept up a barrage of correspondence to everyone he thought could influence the decision. And,

bit-by-bit, he won them over. He also proposed a toll on all ships entering Dublin to pay for the building of the new harbour. In addition, he leased 10 acres on Dalkey Hill and offered to provide the granite without charge (over time it nearly bankrupted him!).

In 1815 the Parliament in Britain passed an act 'for the erection of an asylum [harbour] and place of refuge at Dunleary.' A year later the plans for the harbour (with just one pier, the East Pier) were well advanced. The first stone was laid in mid-1817 under the direction of engineer John Rennie. But he, and others, were worried that a single pier would inevitably become plagued by drifting sandbanks and would provide insufficient protection from northeasterly winds.

The West Pier was approved – a decision which changed the nature of the project from asylum harbour to a fully-fledged port. One problem realised even then but never adequately addressed, was that there was inadequate protection inside the 250-acre harbour from north and northeasterly storms.

Even before the harbour had been decided upon a co-ordinated lifeboat service was set up along the coastline

Dun Laoghaire Harbour

Tom Poole

including, Sandycove (1803), Bullock (1808) and Old Dunleary (1817).

As the harbour walls began to become a reality there was a constant stream of vessels taking advantage of the shelter offered – as many as 1,000 in the first year of construction.

Samuel Lewis, in his Topographical Dictionary (1837) gives a vivid description of the scale of the works. *"The foundation is laid at a depth of 20 feet at low water, and for 14 feet from the bottom of the piers are formed of fine Runcorn stone, in blocks of 50 cubic feet perfectly square; and from 6 feet below water mark to the coping, of granite of excellent quality found in the neighbourhood. They are 310 feet broad at the base and 53 feet on the summit; towards the harbour they are faced with a perpendicular wall of heavy rubble-stone, and towards the sea with huge blocks of granite sloping towards the top at an angle of 10 or 12 degrees."*

In August 1821 the work was visited by King George IV and the burgeoning town was renamed 'Kingstown' in his honour. In 1823 there were 129 men working in the harbour and a further 690 employed in quarrying, shaping, hauling and placing the granite blocks. Labourers and foremen, working a six-day week, were paid 1/8d and 2/- respectively. In 1827 the Harbour Commissioners built a jetty exclusively for the Admiralty's Mail Packets.

In the first year (1834) of the Dublin to Kingstown railway there was an average of 4,000 passengers daily. A year later, even though construction work was still continuing, there were about 2,000 ships (244,282 tons), 57 men-of-war and six daily passenger and mail ferries.

In the 1840s, as yachting became popular, the Royal St. George and the Royal Irish Yacht Clubs were set up and built imposing one-storey buildings. Another, itinerant club, the Royal Alfred, also came into existence around this time. In more recent times they have been joined by the National Yacht Club, originally a rowing club, the Motor Yacht Club, the Sailing Centre and St. Michael's Rowing Club. St. Michael's, founded in the 1920's, recalls a link with the harbour's past when 'hobblers' raced against each other in skiffs to get to incoming ships first with an offer to help them berth.

In 1842, under the direction of Harbour Master William Hutchinson it was decided to build a new pier within the harbour – Traders' Pier. By now the harbour had become the main conduit for mail and passengers into Ireland. Six years later the railway link was completed between London and Holyhead and the 'Irish Mail' rail and boat service came into being. The link with

Tom Roche

Holyhead generated large numbers of passengers, which was good news for Dun Laoghaire as cargo traffic was in decline.

The Carlisle pier replaced Victoria Wharf. By 1859 disembarking passengers had only the shortest of walks to the waiting trains.

The Harbour was also used for prison hulks where prisoners sentenced to transportation were incarcerated in miserable conditions, sometimes for many months, before being taken to Cork for their final voyage from Ireland.

In 1898, the Italian-Irish (his mother, a Jameson, was Irish) scientist Guglielmo Marconi decided to test his newfangled invention, the telegraph, by broadcasting an account of the Royal St. George Yacht Club's annual regatta.

Marconi and his broadcasting equipment accompanied the race aboard a steam tug. Back onshore, in the Dun Laoghaire Harbour Office (now Moran Park House), an assistant transcribed the incoming Morse code before passing the details to a reporter.

Though the day was foggy and those on shore could see little, Marconi managed to collect a clear description of the race.

On the 100th anniversary of the broadcast a plaque was unveiled in Moran Park with his daughter, Princess Elettra, present.

In 1963 work began on an extraordinary undertaking, the construction in the harbour of a vast concrete base and tower (25,000 tons, base of 104 ft diameter, tower 101 ft high), which would replace the lightships at the Kish Bank. The first base had to be abandoned after being deliberately sunk during a storm, but on June 30 1965 the giant structure was towed from the harbour.

1995 saw the opening of the new Stena terminal on the Carlisle Pier and the arrival of a new type of transport, the HSS. One of the largest ferries in the world, it is propelled by water jets, has a turnaround time of 30 minutes and carries 1,500 passengers and up to 375 cars. It makes the journey to Holyhead in 99 minutes!

Today Dun Laoghaire Harbour is entering a new phase as a marina and leisure facility under the management of the Dun Laoghaire Harbour Company. A burning question locally is the eventual fate of the Carlisle Pier – the Harbour Company want to create a huge landmark development, others would prefer something smaller.

Tom Roche

Every Christmas Eve, Dun Laoghaire Lifeboat launches to place a wreath on the waters where 15 of its crew perished.

Around 11 a.m. on Christmas Eve, 1895, the *SS Palme* went aground off Merrion Strand. Aboard were a crew of 17, Captain Axel Wiren, his wife and their five-month-old daughter. The Palme caught in storms, made for Kingstown. She missed the harbour mouth and the crew began firing distress signals.

The crew of the lifeboat *Civil Service No. 7* quickly assembled and launched.

As she neared the Palme, a wave caught her and she capsized. She had been designed to right herself, but didn't. Some of the crew managed to haul themselves onto the upturned hull for a time before succumbing to the cold and slipping to the sea.

The wreck came ashore at Merrion Strand on Christmas morning. All hope was finally lost as the bodies drifted to shore. Meanwhile the 20 people on board the Palme 'enjoyed' two further miserable days before being taken off safely.

An inscription on the old lifeboat station reads: *"From this stone boathouse in 1895 in a terrible storm 15 brave men from this lifeboat station rowed out to rescue the crew of a wrecked ship ... Their sacrifice will not be forgotten."*

RMS Leinster

On October 10, 1918, the mail ship RMS Leinster left Kingstown. Twelve miles out she was attacked by the German submarine UB-123. Among the survivors was Chief Special Mechanic J. D. Mason, a U.S. Navy Petty Officer. Two days later he wrote his report:

"At about an hour out from Kingstown I was sitting on the starboard side aft when I heard one of the soldiers shout: "A torpedo". Immediately afterwards ... I saw the second torpedo coming directly for the starboard side.

It was impossible to control the people after the second torpedo hit and there was a rush for the boats and rafts. I lowered myself over the stern with a rope. I swam to a hatch and then to a raft. I looked back and saw the ship sink. There were not more than four or five lifeboats right side up in the water."

Just 10 minutes had passed between the first explosion and the Leinster sinking – taking 501 of the 771 aboard with her. The war ended one month later.

Death off Dun Laoghaire

The good news is that the Maritime Museum should have been re-opened. The bad news is that its finances are parlous and its future uncertain.

Home to the museum is the Mariner's Church (1835) on Haigh Terrace, a venue which is both historically apt and economically disastrous.

The closure came after the Museum was told not to admit the public. It wasn't an unreasonable order as the premises had no smoke or fire alarms, no back-up lighting and electrical wiring which probably should have been on display rather than in use. And then storms blew in some of the stained-glass windows. As the building is a listed structure these had to be restored to their original condition. Not forgetting the roof: over 500,000 Euro is needed to repair it.

The Maritime Museum is owned and run by the Maritime Institute of Ireland. As a volunteer group, it is not in a position to meet these recurring financial dramas, but people like Des Branigan and Dr. John de Courcy Ireland, two of the founders of the Institute (1941), are used to the uphill struggle.

"We are committed to staying in Dun Laoghaire and the town keeps telling us that it wants it that way," says Des Branigan, President of the Institute. *"Unfortunately that has never translated into grants or even into volunteers to keep the Museum open."*

He believes strongly that the Carlisle Pier would make an ideal location for the Maritime Museum – not a view shared by the Harbour Company. *"Whatever the Harbour Company says, the truth is that it is a decision for the Minister. Handing over the pier to the local authority would not cost the Minister a penny,"* he argues.

The Museum came into being from gifts received by the Institute over the years. Today the highlights include the massive Baily Optic (the 1902 light from the lighthouse in Howth), items from *RMS Leinster* and Isambard Kingdom Brunel's *Great Eastern*, a model of the *Sirius* (the first steam ship to cross the Atlantic) and a display tracing the history of the Irish naval service from before Independence to the present day.

"Always overlooked is one of the most important features, our library," says Des. It contains 4,000 volumes on marine affairs, some of them dating back to the 16th century.

Museum of the Maritime Institute of Ireland

At the back of the children's playground in the People's Park there is an outcrop of rock – the sole reminder of the quarry which was once there.

The Kingstown Commissioners bought the quarry for £500 from the Board of Works in 1889. They obtained a £4,000 Local Government Board loan to develop the two hectares (four acres) as a place where local people could relax. A local architect, J. L. Robinson, who also designed the Town Hall, old Post Office and St. Michael's Hospital, was employed to draw up plans for a formal park with a bandstand and fountains.

The quarry was filled in and the Martello Tower, which stood at the site of the children's playground, was demolished and used as infill. A section of the Tower's gun battery now forms part of the structure of Dun Laoghaire Baths (on the seafront opposite the People's Park). Originally the park was planted with elm trees which are suited to sea exposure. Killed off by Dutch Elm disease they have been replaced with horse chestnut and sycamore.

The gates were bought for £424 and the two fountains were purchased from the Sun Foundry, Glasgow. One fountain was restored in 1985 and given a plaque to commemorate the Easter Rising, the second was restored in 1988 three years later as part of Dun Laoghaire's contribution to the Dublin Millennium Year.

On September 29, 1990, the 100th anniversary of the opening day, a special ceremony was held to rededicate the bandstand. Present on the day were several descendants of J. L. Robinson. Dun Laoghaire Borough Historical Society members planted an oak – a practice which has been continued with various local commemorative plantings, also marked the anniversary.

The Park contains a number of memorials, including one to those who died in the atomic bombings of Hiroshima and Nagasaki.

The People's Park

In 1804 Napoleon Bonaparte was on the prowl and Britain felt vulnerable to attack at home and abroad.

Ten years earlier a British naval assault on a fortified tower at Cape Mortella, Corsica (by coincidence the birthplace of Napoleon), had proved surprisingly difficult. Even though lightly defended, it held two warships at bay, setting one on fire, killing 62 men, and forcing both ships to retreat. It only surrendered to shore artillery when red-hot shot ignited the heavy lining in the parapet.

In 1804 it was decided to build copies - without the inflammable lining – and by the end of the Napoleonic Wars there were Martello Towers in the East Indies, Canada and Ireland.

In Dublin the forts were positioned along the coast about a quarter of a mile apart – each was visible to another on either side so signals could be exchanged. Though not identical, each 40 ft. tower contained three storeys – stores at the base, living quarters above, and a rooftop containing a long-range 24-pounder cannon with a range of one mile on a traversing carriage. The parapet, about four feet high contained loopholes through which a carronade could be fired – a close quarter weapon which delivered a load of shrapnel. Of the four built in Dun Laoghaire area, only two survive, the most famous of which is at Sandycove.

Oliver St. John Gogarty moved into Sandycove Tower in 1904 and, in September, he was joined by James Joyce. Seven days later Joyce moved out after another visitor, Samuel Chevenix Trench, in the middle of a bad dream about a leopard, reached for his gun, fired a few shots, and promptly went back to sleep. Gogarty, it is said, grabbed the gun and fired further shots over Joyce's head. A shaken Joyce moved out the following day. His time in the tower was not forgotten – it became the setting for the opening of *Ulysses*.

In 1962, the James Joyce Museum was opened there by Silvia Beach, publisher of *Ulysses*. The collection includes a death mask of James Joyce, letters, first and rare editions, personal possessions and photographs. The second floor replicates the sleeping quarters shared by Gogarty, Trench and Joyce.

The Joyce Tower

Every June 16, Bloomsday, Glasthule is the local hub, along with nearby Sandycove, for the annual celebration of James Joyce's *Ulysses* and its principal character, Leopold Bloom.

Glasthule and Sandycove are so closely linked that they share a common Residents' Association. To know exactly where Sandycove ends and Glasthule begins is the mark of a true native of the area!

The name is derived from a small stream (Glas) and Tuathail (the surname Toole). People who wrongly think they've originated the association often vulgarly link it with Stillorgan and Ballsbridge.

Until the start of the 19th century Glasthule village had a small population and stood in splendid rural isolation in 'The Land's End', the name given to the area between Dun Laoghaire and Sorrento. The arrival of the harbour and the railway spurred a building boom right across the coastal area and Glasthule was no exception. By 1837 a Mr. Quinn was on hand at Dun Laoghaire railway station to bring travellers to Bray – the trip to Glasthule costing 6d.

During the Civil War, Volunteer James Hudson, from Dun Laoghaire, was killed in action in Glasthule on August 17, 1922. He is buried in the Republican Plot, Deansgrange Cemetery.

Today the area is best known for its fine food - journalists and TV presenters feel morally bound to include Caviston's delicatessen and restaurant whenever a programme includes the word 'gourmet.' The Eagle House pub is a central landmark in the area and nearby Fitzgerald's is also well known.

Literary links to the area include poet and playwright Padraic Colum who was educated at Glasthule national school, dramatist John Millington Synge, writer and playwright Hugh Leonard who received a scholarship to Presentation College Glasthule, and local writer Jamie O'Neill whose first novel *At Swim, Two Boys* (2001) is largely set in the area:

'Glasthule, homy old parish, on the lip of Dublin Bay. You could see the bay, a wedge of it, between the walls of a lane, with Howth lying out beyond. The bay was blue as the sky, a tinge deeper, and curiously raised-looking when viewed dead on. The way the sea would be sloping to the land.'

Glasthule

Dalkey is one of Ireland's Heritage Towns, a status reserved for those few places in Ireland which have managed to preserve some part of their original structure in the face of modernisation.

It is a Norman town, though the church of St. Begnet, which adjoins Goat Castle, dates back to the 7th century. The castle takes its name from the Cheevers family, one of the great landowners in olden times. The castle houses a Heritage Centre, with a small museum containing local artefacts and models of the Atmospheric Railway and the Quarry. It is overpriced for what it offers and also denies free access to St. Begnet's Church.

Across the road stands Archbold's Castle (closed to the public). These two Castles are all that remain of the original seven fortified warehouses where English and French traders stored their wares from the 14th to the 16th century. To defend against raids by the O'Byrnes and the O'Tooles the town was once walled and there was a ditch to make it more difficult for pillagers to escape with heavy goods or cattle.

Dalkey fell into gentle decline when shipping moved to Ringsend at the end of the 16th century. It was not until quarrying began for the building of Dun Laoghaire Harbour in the early 19th century that the good times returned. But it was the arrival of the railway (1843) which saw the building boom in the area which created the town as it is today.

If you take a look at the top storey of the Queens' pub beside Goat Castle you'll see that the windows are false, just painted on the plasterwork. This was a result of a window tax over two centuries ago!

Close by, if you keep an eye on the ground, you can see the tramlines leading into the Tramyard and the emblem of the tramway company on the gates.

Dalkey is that kind of town; the bits and pieces that make it special are in front of you.

Alice Cullen, a local historian, gives regular guided tours around Dalkey and Killiney (details can be found on www.dalkeyhomepage.ie – the best local area website in Dublin).

Dalkey Island (Thorn Island) takes its name either from the 'Deilgei' (Norse) or 'Delginis' (Irish).

It has several springs of fresh water and one of them, on the western side, was in the past considered to have healing properties, particularly for the cure of scurvy and skin diseases.

Dalkey Island has always been a place of refuge. According to the *Annals of the Four Masters*, Sedgha, a Milesian chieftain of great renown erected a fort there and evidence has been found of a promontory fort. In 938 Coibhdeanach, Abbot of Cillachoidh, was drowned nearby while fleeing from the Norsemen; and in 942 the few Danes who escaped from Dublin, when the Irish destroyed it, fled to the island in ships. In 1575 Dalkey Island once more became a refuge for Dublin citizens fleeing from an outbreak of plague in the city.

North of the island are three small rocky islets – Lamb Island, Clare Rock and Maiden Rock – and to the north-east is the group of rocks known as the Muglins, on which, in 1766, were hung in chains, the bodies of the pirates MacKinley and Gidley, who were executed for the murder of Captain Cochrane, Captain Glass and other passengers of the ship *Sanwich*, on the high seas in the previous year.

For some years up to 1797 (the rebellion in the following year put a halt to any further 'politicking', however humorously intended) the island was the scene of the annual coronation of the King of Dalkey, presided over in this instance by *"His facetious Majesty, Stephen the First, King of Dalkey, Emperor of the Muglins, Prince of the Holy Island of Magee, Elector of Lambay and Ireland's Eye, Defender of his own faith and Respecter of all others, Sovereign of the illustrious Order of the Lobster and Periwinkle."* The festivities have occasionally been recreated but have never since proved as popular.

In the 19th century there was a proposal to build a prison there, and when Napoleon's invasion was feared the Martello Tower had an additional guard of troops and a few small guns.

Today Dalkey Island is uninhabited, though busy enough on a summer day as visitors retrace the steps of the Kings of Dalkey.

Dalkey Island

Killiney has for long been one of the most popular, and expensive, parts of Dublin in which to live.

The name comes from the Irish Cill Íníon Léine, the church of the daughter(s) of Léine. It once belonged to the Priory of the Holy Trinity in Dublin and in the 14th century, it was inhabited by John Milis, and many cottagers, who were bound to carry out 'divers works' on the farm of the Priory and who had to supply 15 reapers at harvest-time.

When Henry VIII took the old monasteries apart, Killiney passed through a number of hands including the owners of Loughlinstown, the Goodmans. Their property was seized after the Rebellion of 1641 and was, at the restoration of the monarchy, given to the Church of Ireland.

The area has evidence (both real and possibly manufactured) of early habitation. Towards the close of the 18th century Mr. Peter Wilson, a Dalkey businessman, retired to Killiney and built himself 'a neat lodge' close to the ruined church (Marino Avenue). It was on his land that the monuments (which may later have become the 'Druid's Chair') were found. There is dispute as to whether the 'Druid's Chair' is historic or a Victorian folly, perhaps created from the stones of an ancient monument.

The debate has never been resolved but for many years it was included on maps as a 'Pagan Temple.'

In the year 1831 a stone coffin, containing a perfect skeleton and numerous ancient coins (Saxon and Danish), was found by a ploughman in a field near Killiney called Quatre Bras which then belonged to a Captain Richardson.

One piece of bad news for Dubliners in early 2003 was the decision of the Killiney Court Hotel to apply for planning permission to convert into apartments. With the Dalkey Island Hotel now but a memory it is a pity that the Court Hotel with its fine views seems fated also to disappear.

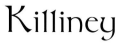

Killiney

On a sunny day, there are few places in Dublin better suited to stretching the legs, or just having a quiet nap, than Killiney Hill (480 ft.). Whether you choose to view the surrounding county from the base of the obelisk or take a leisurely stroll through the trees, it's a haven of peace where it's easy to forget the pace of life in modern Dublin.

F. E. Ball, one of the great writers on Dublin, wrote: -

'On reaching the Obelisk, we obtain what is probably the finest coast view in the county. Two marble slabs on the side facing the sea bear the inscriptions: -
"Last year being hard with the Poor, the Walls about these Hills and This [Obelisk] erected by John Mapas, Esq, June, 1742."
"Repaired by Robert Warren, Esq., MDCCCXL."'

William Bulfin, however, was not impressed:–

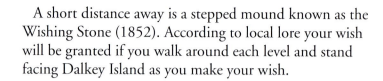

'A monument stands there which is an architectural monstrosity and a vainglorious abomination. ... The model chosen by the designer seems to have been the sawed-off stump of a candlestick surmounted by an extinguisher. Its ugliness is outlandish.'

A short distance away is a stepped mound known as the Wishing Stone (1852). According to local lore your wish will be granted if you walk around each level and stand facing Dalkey Island as you make your wish.

Only a few yards away but partly obscured by foliage is a third obelisk, inscribed Mount Mapas, of which little is known. John Mapas is known to have left money for a memorial and this could be it.

The Telegraph Tower or Castle above Dalkey Quarry was built in 1807 as a signalling station to communicate with the Martello Towers along the coast and with ships in the bay. Later it stored explosives for blasting in the quarries below. Even a quick examination of the quarry gives a good idea of the huge amount of stone which was removed – forever changing the aspect of Killiney Hill.

The park was once part of the estate of Killiney Castle (now Fitzpatrick's Castle Hotel) a prominent residence in the district. The park was bought for £5,000 from Robert Warren Jnr. by Queen Victoria's Golden Jubilee Memorial Association and was formally opened as a public park on June 30, 1887, by Prince Albert Victor.

Killiney Hill

Tom Roche

Headlines From History

Most people like a story of murder, mayhem and madness and over the years this area of Dublin has produced its fair share. There follows a selection of such tales, some of them related to articles in the main section (the O'Connor family tragedy ties in, for example, with the Dun Laoghaire Pumping Station piece), and some which stand alone. I've tried to write them with gusto and accuracy – it's the tabloid journalist within me and these were the tabloid stories of the day.

The First Modern Olympics

One day in 1789 posters appeared all over Dublin inviting all and sundry to 'a great Olympic pig hunt,' at Fiat Hill, a property next door to Temple Hill, the magnificent home of Lord Clonmell.

The organiser was John Magee, publisher of the Dublin Evening Post, who bore a long-running grudge against Clonmell and had £4,000 to spend on revenge. Clonmell, a judge, had jailed Magee some time before. Even the name of the Magee's house was significant – 'Fiat' means an arbitrary and unjust decision.

Magee invited all his friends, 'known and unknown, washed and unwashed' and promised various field sports, with plenty of Silvester Costigan's whisky. Several thousand people took up the offer.

A neighbour, Lord Cloncurry, wrote:

"I recollect attending, and the fete certainly was a strange one. Several thousand people, including the entire disposable mob of Dublin of both sexes, assembled as the guests at an early hour, and proceeded

to enjoy themselves in tents and booths erected for the occasion.

A variety of sports was arranged for their amusement, such as climbing poles for prizes, running races in sacks, grinning through horse-collars, and so forth, until at length, when the crowd had attained its maximum density towards the afternoon, the grand scene of the day was produced.

A number of active pigs, with their tails shaved and soaped, were let loose, and it was announced that each pig was to become the property of any one who could catch and hold it by the slippery member.

A scene impossible to describe immediately took place: the pigs, frightened and hemmed in by the crowd in all other directions, rushed through the hedge which then separated the grounds of Temple Hill from the open fields; forthwith all their pursuers followed in a body, and, continuing their chase over the shrubberies and parterres, soon revenged John Magee upon the noble owner."

It's all a gas ...

Even as the railway came to Dun Laoghaire there were plans to extend it to Dalkey, Killiney and Bray. As the parent line had proved itself a success it seems only human perversity could result in the building of a completely separate and radically different type of railway – one which was more expensive to build and to run, was separate from the existing line, and which never turned a profit!

But it must be remembered that many scientists and engineers thought at the time that the steam railway was only a temporary solution. They pinned their hopes on an Atmospheric Railway – based on the well-known scientific fact that nature abhors a vacuum.

A stationary engine was used to create a vacuum in a cylindrical pipe laid between ordinary rail tracks. A piston connected one carriage on each train to the vacuum cylinder. An ingenious fat-soaked leather flap on the cylinder was used to maintain air-tightness and vacuum pressure. The vacuum principle was used only between Dun Laoghaire and Dalkey, reverse journeys relying on gravity for propulsion.

Work on the new line began on Monday, September 26, 1842, and on August 19, 1843, the first atmospheric train ran and the official opening came on March 29, 1844. Unusually there was provision only for second and third class passengers.

It differed in several ways from the steam railway. It was swift, silent, safe, there was no billowing smoke and collisions were impossible as only one train could occupy a section at a time. However if, for any reason, a train broke down another could not go to the rescue. And, if the Dalkey pumping station broke down, the entire line stopped until it was repaired. There were also continual problems with the leather flaps, which became a delicacy for local rats.

The success of steam locomotives meant that time ran out for Atmospheric locomotion and the line was closed for conversion on April 12, 1854. A relic remains in the name Atmosphere Road.

"I have a dream..."

In 1834 Dalkey was the scene of a remarkable gold rush.

Etty Scott, the beautiful and misty-eyed daughter of a Scottish quarryman, one of many squatters who had built rough cabins near the shore, dreamt that vast quantities of treasure, looted by the Danes, was buried nearby under the 'Long Rock' near the shore. In the middle of October she shared her vision with other quarrymen and Dalkey natives. Within a short time the hidden gold was the talk of the town.

A meeting was held on the Commons, a council of goldfinders formed and thirty-six men began blasting night after night and day after day, watched by thousands of curious onlookers.

"Watch well – work with energy! But, above all, believe in my dream," Etty told her believers. *"The secreted treasure of the Dane will be surely found if you to hearken to my voice."*

A month passed but nothing was found. Etty grimly urged her workers on, but there were some who thought the farce had gone far enough. A group met one evening in Dalkey and hatched a fiendish plan.

Two black cats had long cords with sponges dipped in turpentine attached to their tails, and then their bodies were rubbed with dry phosphorus. They were transported silently to where the work was continuing and lit matches were applied.

An account reads: –

'In a few minutes, strange spectral visions presented themselves in the surrounding darkness, springing and flying from rock to rock, in all directions. The miners stood aghast in groups … feline screams and mewlings were echoed through the night. They felt as if they were invited to revel with the hideous ghoul of the place.'

All save Etty fled and the gold rush was over.

As for Etty, Gaskin writes in Irish Varieties, *'The broken-hearted gold-dreamer of Dalkey sickened and died.'*

There was, however, a happier ending for some of the squatters when people who had come out of curiosity decided to purchase plots for houses on the shore. Landmania broke out and thousands of pounds were paid for what had, just a few months before, been considered worthless ground.

Among the impressive residences built in the aftermath of the Dalkey Gold Rush were Coliemore Lodge, Lota, Elsinore and Cliff Castle.

'Sir' Davy Stephens (1843-1925)

For many years from the mid-19th to the early 20th centuries 'Sir' Davy Stephens, newspaper seller, wit and racing fan, jealously guarded the Harbour. The longhaired news-vendor became a local celebrity as he met each vessel.

His normal post was at the steps to the Railway station, even the Post Office accepted this as his address, but he would charge up the gangway of each ship as soon as it was lowered bearing copies of *The Irish Times*, *The Freeman's Journal*, and *The Lady of the House*.

In 1882 he was 'knighted' by the then Lord Lieutenant, Lord Spencer. Davy, it appears, had gone down on bended knee to present him with the papers and Spencer smote him on the shoulder and announced "Arise, Sir Davy Stephens!" Though only a joke, the 'Sir' stuck with Davy forever more!

The only times of the year when Davy went missing

in action were for the Punchestown Races and the Ascot Derby when he boarded a City of Dublin Steam Packet Co. steamer, to return a week later.

On one such return, after 52 years of newspaper selling, Davy was banished from Carlisle Pier and replaced by *"a chap with gold lace on his cap selling papers in my place."* The matter was raised by Michael Davitt in Parliament and Davy was eventually allowed to resume his gangway position.

Davy also contributed 'Davy's Kolum' in the *Kingstown Monthly* (1894) and produced a small 'autobiography' which he sold himself. It is long-winded, muddled and occasionally funny. The following ditty comes from it:

> *Davy hath a beaming eye,*
> *On all his customers it beameth;*
> *Everyone who passes by*
> *Thinks that for himself it gleameth.*
> *But there's an eye that's brighter far,*
> *And shines behind this jovial quizziness,*
> *Leading like a guiding star,*
> *And that is Davy's eye to business.*

Death by seafood

Most people today have never heard of James O'Connor of Blackrock. But in 1890 the tragedy, which befell his family, was much more than a seven-day wonder.

O'Connor was a journalist on the staff of the *United Ireland* paper and lived with his family at 1 Seapoint Avenue. On the evening of June 30 his children had been out on the strand and had brought home some mussels they had picked. The family and a servant, Lizzie Casey, ate some of them and within minutes were experiencing terrible pains.

When Mr. O'Connor arrived home, just 20 minutes or so after the mussels had been eaten, he immediately administered an emetic to them all and a neighbour was sent to get two doctors, Dixon and Finucane, from Blackrock. Both were on the scene shortly but could do little to prevent Mrs. Mary ('Molly') O'Connor, and her daughters Annie, 13, Aileen, 11, and Kathleen, 7, from death. Another daughter, Norah, 5, lingered for a few hours before she, too, died. The only survivors of the meal of mussels were the servant and a daughter, Moya (Moyra) who had eaten only a very small amount.

The Freeman's Journal gave a full account of the tragedy, concluding: *'To leave his family in the possession of health and to come back in a few hours to his home and find all struggling with a painful death is a terrible experience.'*

The inquest was held the day after the deaths and clear evidence was shown that the mussels had come from a pond, which had been condemned 15 years before. The coroner, Mr. Davys, noted: *'The fault lay with the Town Commissioners for not having provided a sewer.'*

James O'Connor was later elected an MP in 1892, a position he held until his death in 1910. His daughter, Moya, was later friendly with Michael Collins and was imprisoned during the War of Independence. She died in 1944.

Falling from grace

A family which had, over 150 years, built up a reputation for honesty and integrity was destroyed by a man who singularly failed to live up to the family motto of 'Sans Tache' (Without Stain).

That man was Frank DuBédat who, in 1889, was head of the family and of the successful Dublin stockbrokers and bankers, William George DuBédat and Sons of Foster Place (now the Bank of Ireland Arts' Centre).

That year he began work on 'Frankfort' (now Kenah Hill), a magnificent house and estate in Killiney. It, like Frank, was aimed at reflecting a public image of success, respectability and substance. He was an imposing figure, five feet nine or ten and over 20 stone. He was influential, charming, respected – and a thief.

He had fraudulently taken money from clients and, through extravagant living and failed investments, had lost it all. He had also developed a liking for the theatrical world and travelled regularly to Paris.

In October 1890 he became President of the Dublin Stock Exchange. Even as he was sworn in he knew that exposure could only be a matter of time but, ever an optimist, he held on until the last possible moment.

On Christmas Eve 1890 he wrote letters to his wife, Rosie, from London and promptly disappeared. Within days the family firm had collapsed with debts of over

£100,000 and he was struck off the list of members of the Dublin Stock Exchange.

Six months later he was arrested in Capetown, South Africa, and sent back to Dublin where, after a one-day trial, he was sentenced to 12 months hard labour and seven years penal servitude.

The judge remarked: *"You chose to make a rush for riches and the race for greed, as so often happens, has ended in ruin for yourself, bitter memories to others and benefit to none."*

Frank, however, must have had some redeeming features, for among the petitions calling for his early release was one containing the names of his former Killiney employees.

Given early release in 1896, he returned to South Africa, was imprisoned again and received an unconditional discharge. He spent his final years as a recluse.

Queen Victoria drops in

The news that Queen Victoria was to visit Dublin in 1900 came as somewhat of a surprise, details only being released three weeks before she arrived.

Michael F. J. McCarthy wrote at the time:

'When the Victoria and Albert, having her Majesty on board, dropped anchor, amidst the booming of a hundred cannon, in the middle of Kingstown harbour, at quarter past two in the afternoon of Tuesday, the 3rd of April, the city of Dublin and its horseshoe of environs from Howth to Killiney, and its beautiful bay enclosed within the arms of that horseshoe, presented an appearance of rejoicing and expectation never before equalled. When night fell, the beautiful town of Kingstown, which slopes up so picturesquely from the water level, was illuminated...'

On the following day, about half-past eleven, she landed at Victoria Wharf (now St. Michael's), and met with the great and the good in a specially erected pavilion. *"I am very pleased to find myself in Ireland once more,"* she said.

McCarthy was again on hand:

'Sailors and soldiers, with military bands at numerous points, lined the nine miles of road from the wharf to the Viceregal Lodge. Bunting of every description bedecked the highways. But better than naval or military display, were the kindly faces of innumerable Irish, men women and children who came out to see the Queen.'

On her final departure from Dun Laoghaire, on April 26, she wore a large bunch of shamrocks on her breast. *"I am very sorry to leave Ireland. I have had an extremely pleasant time,"* she was quoted as saying in the *Irish Times*.

Before she left, she conferred baronetcies on the Lord Mayors of Dublin and Belfast – T. W. Robinson, chairman of the Kingstown Township Board, had to wait until May 24 (Queen Victoria's birthday) for a knighthood.

Ac the bar...

The National Union of Vintners, Grocers and Allied Trade Assistants (now part of the trade union Mandate) has two particularly strong links to Dun Laoghaire.

Patrick Moran, an IRA Dublin Brigade Captain and President of the Dublin area of the union, was executed on March 14, 1921, for his part in the killing of British secret agents. Strong evidence was produced that he could not have been involved, but to no avail. Moran Park is named after him.

The second connection has a hint of farce about it and led to an entry in the Guinness Book of Records.

W.W.II started in 1939 and so did a strike at Downey's public house in central Dun Laoghaire (demolished when the Shopping Centre was being built), which was to outlast the war by eight years.

The owner, Jim Downey, lived on Northumberland Avenue, and was generally considered a kind and generous man. But he wasn't going to back down, and neither were the strikers.

As the strike went on, and on, the pub became a local tourist attraction. The initial bitterness broke down and Downey was known to bring out hot drinks and clear snow from the path during bad winters. In return, it was not unknown for strikers, to help eject troublemakers.

The strike was only resolved in 1953 when Jim Downey died. During the 14 years it was estimated that the strikers walked over 41,000 miles.

Sally Farrelly remembers a piece of doggerel, *Two Worries*, that hung in the window for many years

"During your life you've two worries, whether you're going to live or whether you're going to die..."

And so it proved.

Read on...

∽

There are many books which provide greater details about the area and more are being added every year. The following is a brief introduction to some which are readily available.

Perhaps the most respected book on the area is *Between the Mountains and the Sea* by Peter Pearson. Published by The O'Brien Press in 1999 it has been twice updated and reprinted. It is particularly strong on architecture and contains hundreds of illustrations.

Photographically, there is nothing to compare with Christian Corlett's *Antiquities of Old Rathdown* published in 1999 by Wordwell Limited. If you've ever wanted to know more about dolmens, high crosses and castles, this book is a must.

The History of Dun Laoghaire Harbour, by John de Courcy Ireland, published by De Búrca, chronicles the events which have shaped the harbour as it moved from being a trading port to leisure amenity.

A wider area than might be expected from the title is covered by *The Town of the Road – the story of Booterstown* by Hazel P. Smyth, published by Pale Publishing.

The *Dictionary of Irish Biography*, by Henry Boylan, published by Gill & Macmillan, is a mine of information about famous Irish people, as is *Dublin's Famous People*, by John Cowell, published by O'Brien Press.

The Dun Laoghaire Borough Historical Society produces an annual Journal which is available locally, priced 5 Euro. Some back issues (p&p 1 Euro within Ireland) are available from the Society which has also published *The Historical Street Directory of Dun Laoghaire/Kingstown* and a history of the Pavilion, *The Story of the Pavillion*.

The Blackrock Society publishes an annual selection of articles and photographs which, though not exclusively dealing with matters historical or local, provides much information about the area. Details of the Society are available from 5 Idrone Terrace, Blackrock.

The Genealogical Society of Ireland, 11 Desmond Avenue, Dun Laoghaire, has published several volumes on genealogical sources, memorial inscriptions from local graveyards, etc. Full details are available online at www.gensocireland.org. The Society is currently restoring the Martello Tower, Seapoint, for use as an Archive and as a free genealogical research centre for Ireland.

Acknowledgements

∞

When I took on the job of writing this book I didn't give it much thought. 'A piece of cake,' was my initial response. After all, there can't be much to writing a book, can there?

I wrong! If it wasn't for the help given to me by everyone I approached, you wouldn't be reading this and I'd probably be on the run from a vengeful Tim Johnston of Cottage Publications.

Both myself and the artist Tom Roche worked very closely and amiably together from start to finish. It was great fun teasing out our route.

I would like to especially thank Livinus Killen, my friend, proof-reader and sounding-board. If you like what you have read it is largely down to him.

Also, Jane Crosbie, Cottage Publications, who put some of my more strangulated sentences into English.

Both Colin Scudds and Brian Smith Dun Laoghaire Borough Historical Society, and Michael Merrigan, Genealogical Society of Ireland, went out of their way to help me. If anyone can prove to me that St. Patrick has any link with Dun Laoghaire it will be Michael Merrigan!

Councillor Jane Dillon-Byrne has been a friend for many years and without her the article on public sculpture would not have been possible.

When I had written myself into a corner in Dalkey and could think of no way out, one was provided by Alice Cullen.

The article on public houses is the result of many years of personal research during which I have paid at least one visit to every pub in the area covered. It's a dirty job, but somebody had to do it! In-depth research continues to be carried out at Bakers Corner, Kill o'the Grange; Dunphy's, Lower George's Street, Dun Laoghaire, and O'Rourke's, Blackrock.

For some reason Flann O'Brien plays a larger part than I had ever envisaged – if you haven't read his books you've missed one of the great comic writers.

As my living-room descended into the abyss of clutter, with books strewn everywhere – and I do mean everywhere – my wife, Anne, showed admirable restraint. Without her encouragement and belief in my ability to finish it, I'd still be floundering.

Finally, my thanks to Tim Johnston for offering me the chance to write this book and to you for reading this far – I hope it's been enjoyable.

Ken Finlay

Dear Reader

This book is from our much complimented illustrated book series which includes:-

Belfast
By the Lough's North Shore
East Belfast
South Belfast
Antrim, Town & Country
Inishowen
Donegal Highlands
Donegal, South of the Gap
Donegal Islands
Fermanagh
Omagh
Cookstown
Dundalk & North Louth

Drogheda & the Boyne Valley
Blanchardstown, Castleknock and the Park
Dundrum, Stillorgan & Rathfarnham
Blackrock, Dún Laoghaire, Dalkey
Limerick's Glory
Galway on the Bay
The Book of Clare
Armagh
Ring of Gullion
The Mournes
Heart of Down
Strangford Shores

For the more athletically minded our illustrated walking book series includes:-

Bernard Davey's Mourne   Tony McAuley's Glens
Bernard Davey's Mourne Part 2

Also available in our 'Illustrated History & Companion' Range are:-

City of Derry   Holywood   Ballymoney
Lisburn   Banbridge

And from our Music series:-

Colum Sands, Between the Earth and the Sky

We can also supply prints, individually signed by the artist, of the paintings featured in the above titles as well as many other areas of Ireland.

For details on these superb publications and to view samples of the paintings they contain, you can visit our web site at www.cottage-publications.com or alternatively you can contact us as follows:-

Telephone: +44 (028) 9188 8033   Fax: +44 (028) 9188 8063

Cottage
Publications

Cottage Publications
is an imprint of
Laurel Cottage Ltd
15 Ballyhay Road
Donaghadee, Co. Down
N. Ireland, BT21 0NG